Sudan

By Charles Piddock

Academic Consultant: Abraham Marcus
Associate Professor
Department of History and Center for Middle Eastern Studies
University of Texas at Austin

WORLD ALMANAC® LIBRARY

Please visit our Web site at: www.garethstevens.com
For a free color catalog describing World Almanac® Library's list of high-quality books
and multimedia programs, call 1-800-848-2928 (USA) or 1-800-387-3178 (Canada).
World Almanac® Library's fax: (414) 332-3567

Library of Congress Catalog-in-Publication Data

Piddock, Charles.
    Sudan / by Charles Piddock.
        p. cm. — (Nations in the news)
    Includes bibliographical references and index.
    ISBN-10: 0-8368-6711-4 — ISBN-13: 978-0-8368-6711-4 (lib. bdg.)
    ISBN-10: 0-8368-6718-1 — ISBN-13: 978-0-8368-6718-3 (softcover)
    1. Sudan—Juvenile literature.   I. Title.   II. Series: Piddock, Charles. Nations in the news.
    DT154.6.P534   2007
    962.4—dc22   2006011218

First published in 2007 by
World Almanac® Library
A Member of the WRC Media Family of Companies
330 West Olive Street, Suite 100
Milwaukee, WI 53132 USA

A Creative Media Applications, Inc. Production
Writer: Charles Piddock
Design and Production: Alan Barnett, Inc.
Editor: Susan Madoff
Copy Editor: Laurie Lieb
Proofreaders: Laurie Lieb and Donna Drybread
Indexer: Nara Wood
World Almanac® Library editorial direction: Mark J. Sachner
World Almanac® Library editor: Gini Holland
World Almanac® Library art direction: Tammy West
World Almanac® Library production: Jessica Morris

Photo credits: Associated Press: cover photo, pages 5, 7, 8, 9, 12, 13, 16, 19, 35, 37, 39, 41, 43;
Landov: pages 14, 18; New York Public Library, Astor, Lenox and Tilden Foundations: pages 20, 23, 26;
Bridgeman Art Library: pages 22, 25, 32; Granger Collection: pages 29, 30; Getty Images: page 34;
maps courtesy of Ortelius Design.

Printed in the United States of America

1 2 3 4 5 6 7 8 9 10 09 08 07 06

Table of Contents

Cover photo: A Sudanese refugee, fleeing political violence in Darfur, Sudan, in July 2004, cries after reaching Bahai on the border of Chad.

A Divided Nation

"Peace in the whole of Sudan is vital, not only for this big country—the biggest in Africa—but for the entire African continent." Javier Solana, the European Union's foreign policy chief, was speaking for the entire world when he spoke these words to reporters during a March 2006 press conference. "We are going to get very serious on Sudan," he said.

While Sudan's recent history has seen almost constant **civil war** between the northern part of the country and

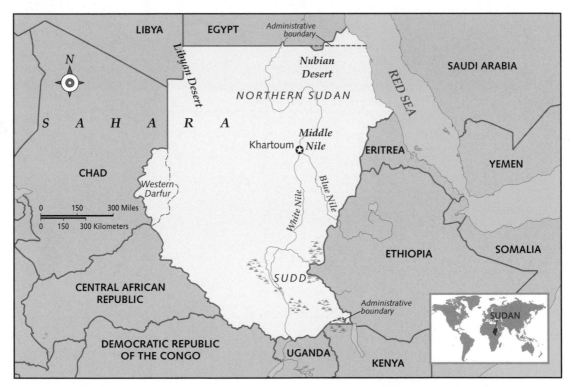

Sudan is bordered by Egypt in the north; Eritrea, Ethiopia, and Kenya in the east; Uganda and the Democratic Republic of the Congo in the south; and the Central African Republic, Chad, and Libya in the west. It is the largest country on the African continent, and its capital is Khartoom.

A sick child lies in her mother's arms as they wait for food and medicine along with many others at a nutrition center in Kalma, Sudan's western Darfur region. The camp is run by the relief organization Doctors Without Borders of Holland.

the southern part, the world's attention now rests on a growing civil war in Sudan's western **province** of Darfur.

Death in Darfur

"Among the stench and the flies, the children lie wasted, staring into space. Tiny human beings, who were born into the madness of man's inhumanity to man, into the madness of a spate of killing that has left many of their fathers, brothers, grandparents and uncles dead," reported Hilary Andersson of the **British**

Broadcasting Corporation (BBC), from a camp for internally displaced people, (IDP), or **refugees** in Darfur, a region of Sudan as large as Texas. "And now, they face starvation which is cruel and slow. Most of the children are too far gone to eat. Some have peeling skin and lesions [open sores] that come with advanced starvation— their skin is wrinkled, loose around the bones. Their mothers sit by powerless."

Andersson's report was in 2004, at the height of the starvation crisis in Darfur. By the end of March 2006, however, little had changed. Darfur continued to be a killing field. The bloody, often confused, and brutal war not only still rages, but has spread. It has left villages and towns **depopulated** and turned farmland into wasteland. It has become a complicated ethnic struggle that pits tribe against tribe, Arab herder against African farmer, and Sudan's government troops against rebels of the Sudan Liberation Army (**SLA**) and the smaller Justice and Equality Movement (**JEM**).

"The Face of Genocide"

Darfur lies near what is often called the "dead heart" of Africa. It is a hot, dry land, with sandy soil and sparse vegetation, buffeted by hot winds from the Sahara, the great desert to the north. By day, African farmers in Darfur struggle to raise their few crops. Night brings not rest, but fear and dread—and often death. The **janjaweed**, or "evil horsemen," often attack at night.

The janjaweed are hooded Arab **militias** that storm into Darfur's farming villages on horses or camels and sometimes in pickup trucks and cars. The janjaweed rape the women, kill the men and boys, steal the livestock, and set the villages and their fields on fire.

In a dispatch to the *New York Times* from Darfur on March 19, 2006, columnist Nicholas Kristof wrote about he calls the "face of genocide" in Darfur:

> The face of genocide I found most searing belonged to Idris Ismael, a 32-year-old Chadian. Mr. Idris said that a Sudan-sponsored janjaweed militia had attacked his village, Damri, that very morning. He had managed to run away. His wife, Halima, eight months pregnant, could only hobble. She was still in the village, along with their four children, ages 3 to 12.
>
> "The village is surrounded by janjaweed, with civilians inside," Mr. Idris said. "There's no way for people to escape. The janjaweed will kill all the men, women and children, take all our blankets and other property, and then burn our homes. They will kill every last person.... The janjaweed will rape and kill my family. And there's nothing I can do."

Omar al-Bashir

Born in January 1944 in a northern Sudanese village, Omar al-Bashir (*shown left*) joined Sudan's army in 1960. He graduated from the Sudan Military Academy in Khartoum in 1966. He came to power in 1989 not in an election, but after an armed **coup** (coo) overthrew the government of Sadiq al-Mahdi. Immediately after taking control, al-Bashir went on Sudanese television to say that the army was taking control of Sudan "to save the country from rotten political parties."

After taking power, al-Bashir proclaimed himself chair of a fifteen-member Revolutionary Command Council for National Salvation (RCC). On behalf of the council, he signed a decree dismissing the elected government and other state bodies. Further decrees by al-Bashir dissolved political parties and trade unions and banned demonstrations against the government. In April 1990, al-Bashir reorganized his government to increase the role of radical **Islamists**. The government was to be strictly based on the Koran, Islam's holy book, not on modern ideas of democracy. In March 1991, al-Bashir's government passed the Criminal Act, which introduced **sharia**, law based on the principles of Islam, in the southern provinces. Five years later, however, in March 1996, the government reintroduced democratic measures and al-Bashir ran for president in nonparty elections. He received nearly 76 percent of the vote. After legalizing political parties in January 1999, al-Bashir was reelected in December 2000 with 86.5 percent of the vote.

President al-Bashir has received praise for working to achieve peace in the south and criticism for supporting the janjaweed and promoting ethnic violence in the western province of Darfur.

Sometimes the janjaweed attack along with Sudan government troops. At other times, they fight against government troops. They also fight other rebel groups. All sides in the conflict have been known to steal and murder to get food or simply to enrich themselves. The confusion and chaos have made it very difficult for international aid organizations to deliver food and medical supplies to those who need them.

The United Nations (UN) reports that more than 1.8 million people in Darfur have been driven from their homes by the violence and that more than 200,000 have fled across the border into eastern Chad. Many of these internally displaced people now live in camps in Darfur and in Chad. In one camp, Kalima, in Sudan, more than 70,000 refugees live in huts made of plastic and mud that stretch 4 miles (6.4 kilometers) across the sandy soil. An estimated 180,000 people have died since 2004 in the Darfur war, many of them from disease or hunger.

The United States and the European Union accuse the Arabs who control Sudan's government of supporting and arming the janjaweed in a deliberate effort to wipe out the black African farmers who support the SLA. U.S. president George W. Bush and secretary of state Condoleezza Rice call

A line of Sudanese women wait to receive food at the Kasab Internally Displaced People's camp in Kutum in northern Darfur in July 2004.

what is happening in Darfur **genocide**. The UN has not officially classified the Darfur war as genocide, but does call it "the world's worst humanitarian crisis" and accuses officials of Sudan's government of war crimes. Sudan's president, Omar al-Bashir, however, strongly rejects the charges and has called the janjaweed "bandits and outlaws."

Spreading Violence

In 2005, the killing in Darfur spread beyond Sudan's borders to neighboring Chad. Kristof of the *New York Times* described what was happening in eastern Chad:

> Militias backed by Sudan race on camels and pickup trucks into Chadian villages and use machine guns to mow down farming families, whose only offense is that they belong to the wrong tribes and have black skin.
>
> I found it eerie to drive on the dirt track along the border because countless villages have been torched or abandoned.... You can drive for mile after mile and see no sign of life—except for the smoke of the villages or fields being burned by the Sudan-armed janjaweed militia.... This is my sixth trip to the Darfur region, and I've often seen burned villages within Darfur itself, but now the cancer has spread to Chad.

An Arab militiaman, a member of janjaweed, is pictured here on horseback in western Darfur, Sudan, in June 2005. The janjaweed are infamous for their violent raids on black African villages, brutally torturing and killing men, women, and children.

As the destruction continues, internally displaced people continue to pour into the IDP camps. The *Christian Science Monitor* reported on one refugee, Jidu Bakr, who led three dozen of his kinsmen to Kalima, walking nearly 100 miles (161 km) in intense heat to escape Arab militias. "It was impossible to live," he told a reporter, "so now we've come here."

Roots of the Conflict

Warfare in Darfur began in February 2003, the result of years of strife between Arab herders and African farmers over the region's scarce resources. When the farmers complained to Sudan's Arab-dominated government about the herders' attacks on their villages, the government reportedly did nothing. Outraged, the African farmers accused the government of unfairly supporting Darfur's Arab minority. Some took up arms in rebellion. In January 2004, after the SLA launched attacks on government targets in the settlements of El-Fasher and Golo in southern Darfur, the government responded with air raids and troops. Many critics charge that the government then enlisted the aid of the janjaweed and other local Arabs to wipe out the entire population of African farmers.

Expansion into Chad

Beginning in 2005, rebels opposed to Chad's government and supported by Sudan's government expanded the war by launching attacks against villages in

Chad from Darfur. Since the rebels' first major attack on the Chad city of Acre in December 2005, the rebel army has grown to nearly ten thousand well-armed men.

To escape the fighting, thousands of Chadians have fled to refugee camps in Sudan. Tensions between Chad and Sudan broke out in fighting between the two countries in 2005, although a cease-fire ended direct confrontation. Chad's government has long supplied the SLA in its fight against Sudan's government. Sudan's government, in turn, has supplied the rebels who are fighting to overthrow Chad's government.

The North-South War

The Darfur conflict has cornered the world's attention, but it has not been the most destructive conflict to tear apart Sudan in recent years. That title belongs to the long civil war between Sudan's Arab north and African south that began in 1956 and only calmed down in 2005.

The southern part of Sudan has been destroyed much like Darfur is being destroyed today, with millions of refugees, abandoned schools, burned villages, ruined roads, collapsed bridges, and a frightening death toll. A UN estimate says that more than two million people have died in the north-south civil war between 1956 and the present.

The long war has some of the same elements as the Darfur conflict. In the north-south conflict, however, religion also plays a major role. Sudan's north is populated by Arab **Muslims**. Almost half of the estimated 22 million Sudanese (no accurate census has taken place in Sudan since 1993 because of the continuing civil wars) are Arabic-speaking Muslims. Most of the people in the south (the provinces of Sudan below the great swamp known as the Sudd) are African and either Christians or **animists**. Animists believe that natural objects and animals contain spirits that can cause harm or create good for people. Christianity in the south is a result of the efforts of Christian **missionaries** who arrived in the region when much of Africa was divided into European colonies. Sudan was ruled jointly as a colony by both Egypt and Great Britain before becoming independent in 1956.

Origins of the War

When Sudan became independent, the Arab- and Muslim-led government in Khartoum, Sudan's capital city, refused to give the south the degree of self-rule promised in Sudan's original constitution. This refusal led to a **mutiny** by southern army officers and to civil war. For the next seventeen years the war raged on and off between north and south.

Sharia

Sharia is the Arabic word for the system of law inspired by the Koran and centuries of interpretation by Muslim scholars. Even though the word *sharia* is almost always translated as "law," sharia is much broader than law. It refers to principles of conduct governing not only religious activities, but also the political, social, and private lives of Muslims.

At the base of sharia are the Five Pillars of Islam, which require all Muslims to *openly declare their faith:* Muslims must say or believe that there is no God but Allah and Muhammad is his prophet.

pray: Muslims pray five times a day—at dawn, noon, mid-afternoon, sunset, and nightfall—reciting verses from the Koran.

give alms: Muslims make donations to charity every year.

fast: Muslims abstain from food and other worldly pleasures from dawn to dusk during the holy month of Ramadan.

go on a pilgrimage: Every adult Muslim who is physically and financially able is expected to make a pilgrimage to the holy city of Mecca once in his or her lifetime.

Sharia also covers many other obligations required of Muslims. Islam is more than just a religion; it is a way of life with rules or obligations governing everything from food and clothing to marriage, education, and politics.

The modernist movement in Islam opposes the traditional view of sharia, which states that the laws of Islam come from God and cannot be changed by humans. Fundamentalist Islamic schools, such as those in Iran, Saudi Arabia, and lately in Sudan, believe in the traditional view. As a result of this difference, Muslims in Iraq, Syria, and Egypt interpret Islamic law regarding women's dress, equality between men and women, and the requirement that men wear beards more loosely than do stricter societies such as Iran and Saudi Arabia. The leaders of Sudan have, in recent years, tended to interpret sharia in accordance with the fundamentalist view, although not as strictly as the leaders of Saudi Arabia or Iran.

After a brief peace in the 1970s, the war erupted again in 1983 when Sudan's president, Gaafar Muhammad al-Nimeiri, declared his intention to turn all of Sudan into a completely Muslim state. He divided the south into three units and imposed sharia on the Christian and animist

An artist in Juba, Sudan, paints a mural of the Sudanese flag with the Arabic words "Yes for Peace and Love" above it in January 2005, while a young boy watches him work. The message on the mural is likely in support of the peace process and an end to violence in the Darfur region.

population. Special police arrested southerners guilty of violating Sharia law.

Angry and upset, the southerners rebelled. A rebel army, the Sudan People's Liberation Army (**SPLA**), took up arms against Sudan's government, and the fighting and killing began again. Much of the south has been destroyed since the resumption of fighting, and more than four million refugees have fled the region, to other parts of Sudan and to other countries in Africa.

An Uncertain Peace

By the spring of 2006, an uneasy peace reigned over southern Sudan. It was the result of a peace agreement signed on January 9, 2005, between the SPLA and the Sudanese government. The two parties agreed to draw up a new Sudanese constitution granting more self-rule to the south. The SPLA leader, John Garang, was to head the southern government and also become a vice president of Sudan itself. Most important, the south would no longer be subject to Sharia law.

Sudan's president, Omar al-Bashir, and John Garang, deadly enemies only months before, signed the peace agreement before an audience of international **dignitaries** in Nairobi, Kenya. Colin Powell, who was then U.S. secretary of state, was in the audience.

Just before President al-Bashir spoke, twenty white doves, symbolizing peace, were released in front of a crowd waving white cloths. Al-Bashir urged the millions of people who had fled the fighting to return home. He promised that new oil wealth found in the south would improve living standards and rebuild the south's **infrastructure**.

Garang, who had led the SPLA for twenty years, told the cheering crowd that the peace deal would change Sudan "forever." The popular SPLA leader, however, was killed in a helicopter crash only three weeks after signing the agreement. He was widely mourned and his death touched off riots. He was replaced by Salva Kiir, who assured mourners that Garang's vision of peace would live on.

The new agreement gives the south six years to decide if it wants to become an independent nation. Juba, always the south's main town, was chosen as the future capital because it is the only town that still has a good paved road.

John Garang

John Garang (*shown left*), the rebel leader turned Sudanese vice president, was considered a hero by many non-Arab Africans. His death in a helicopter crash was mourned throughout the continent.

Garang was born in 1945, a member of the Dinka tribe. His family was Christian and he was sent to study in the United States at Grinnell College, Iowa. After becoming a Sudanese army officer, Garang returned to the United States for military training at Fort Benning, Georgia. In 1983, the Sudanese government sent him to put down a mutiny by five hundred southern troops. Instead of arresting the troops, he joined the mutiny. For the next twenty-two years, he fought as a **guerrilla** against the Sudanese government. The guerrilla war ended in 2005 with Garang and the SPLA achieving most of their objectives.

As a rebel leader, Garang reportedly ruled with an iron hand. He tolerated no disagreements. "John Garang did not tolerate dissent and anyone who disagreed with him or the [SPLA] leadership [was] either imprisoned or killed," says journalist Gill Lusk of *Africa Confidential*. Garang repeatedly survived assassination attempts and outfoxed his opponents for years. He traveled with a collection of bodyguards. Shortly before his death, the SPLA had between fifty thousand and sixty thousand troops, mainly equipped with small arms.

CHAPTER 2

A Large and Varied Country

Sudan is the largest country in Africa in land area. It covers a little over 1 million square miles (2.59 million square km), about one-third the size of the United States. Within its borders exist widely varied climates, from tropical rain forests in the south to bone-dry deserts in the north. Measured rainfall ranges from 40 inches (1,016 millimeters) a year near the Sudd swamp to just about zero inches a year in the desert north of Khartoum.

Geographers divide Sudan into four natural geographic regions. In the north are the Nubian and Libyan deserts, the hottest places in Africa, covering about one-third of the country. Just south of the deserts is an area of grasslands and low hills, covering

Sudanese villagers disembark from a simple boat on the banks of the Nile River in Khartoum, Sudan in September 2004. The White Nile and Blue Nile meet outside the capital city in a tributary called the Athara.

most of central Sudan. Toward the west and east is a series of low mountain ranges running north and south. Down the center of Sudan is the country's main geographical feature: the Nile, the world's longest river, running north for more than 4,000 miles (6,436 km) from deep in the center of Africa to the Mediterranean Sea. The Nile rises in two branches: the White Nile out of Lake Victoria south of Uganda, and the Blue Nile out of the Ethiopian highlands.

The Middle Nile

Geographers use the term *Middle Nile* to describe the region that extends from the joining of the White Nile and Blue Nile at Khartoum to Aswan, in Egypt. This is the part of Sudan where most of the population lives. It is also the area where ancient civilizations in Sudan developed.

The Middle Nile is an extremely arid region that gets almost no rainfall, but it is given life by the river itself. Each year the Nile floods this region, depositing rich soil, most of it brought from Ethiopia by the Blue Nile. The water from the river is used, as it has been for thousands of years, for irrigating farmland. A fertile, cultivated strip lies alongside the river on both sides. Beyond the cultivated strip are vast areas of **savanna** whose inhabitants are nomadic

herders who travel around the area to find food for their animals.

South of the grasslands is Africa's largest swamp, the Sudd. The Sudd covers about 9,000 square miles (23,310 sq km), an area slightly larger than the state of New Hampshire. For thousands of years, the Sudd stood as a barrier between the north and the south in Sudan, blocking the earliest recorded search for the source of the Nile, ordered by the Roman emperor Nero in A.D. 60.

In the Sudd, the Nile flows through tangled channels thick with papyrus reeds. The weedy waters are full of crocodiles and hippopotamuses. There are three main waterways through the Sudd: the Bahr-al-Zaraf ("River of the Giraffes"), Bahr-al-Ghazal ("River of the Gazelles"), and Bahr-al-Jabal ("River of the Mountains"). South of the Sudd stretch the rain forests of central Africa.

Sudan's Ethnic Groups

Sudan's varied geography supports a wide assortment of peoples and cultures. The country contains 19 distinct ethnic groups and 537 subgroups. They speak 143 separate languages divided into 400 dialects. The main division, however, and the main source of Sudan's troubles, is the division between Arab ethnic groups and non-Arab ethnic groups.

Around 39 percent of Sudan's people consider themselves Arabs, but a much larger percentage—maybe as high as 55 percent—speak Arabic and live an Arab way of life. Some of Sudan's Arabs are descendants of Arabs who emigrated to Sudan after the Muslim conquests in the seventh and eighth centuries. Others belong to groups who adopted the Arabic language, Arab culture, and the Muslim religion.

Sudan's Arabs are often of mixed race, but they all share a strong cultural identification with the 250 million Arabic-speaking people who live in the Middle East and elsewhere. Arab identity is closely identified with Arabic language and with Islam, although there are a number of Christian Arabs in the Middle East. Ethnically, Arabs in Sudan are usually darker-skinned than Arabs in the Middle East. Arabic language and culture combine with Islam to influence the way Sudanese Arabs view themselves. They feel that their commitment to these components of their lives separates them from the non-Arab peoples who also live in Sudan.

Most of Sudan's Arabs live in the northern part of Sudan in settled communities. Arab Sudanese dominate Sudan's economy and government.

Members of a tribe of black African Sudanese watch over their herds of cattle in western Darfur in June 2005. Many had fled to Chad in previous months as the janjaweed terrorized the region. Wealthier than most in the region, however, these men were able to purchase weapons and return to Sudan, able to defend themselves and protect their cattle.

Animist religions are the most ancient religions practiced in Sudan. Animists believe that the natural objects around them have power and are able to influence human life in many ways. Many animist groups worship one particular totem, such as a wild animal, a particular tree, or a river, and carefully avoid injuring that object.

Most animist tribes worship their ancestors, believing that their ancestors' spirits must be respected and honored and often prayed to because they have the power to bring harm or good to the family. Because each group respects the rights of other groups to worship their own ancestors, the various animist religions have never been in conflict, although the tribespeople have fought for other reasons.

Many animists also believe in the "evil eye." A bad look from another person with magical power or the help of a witch could cause them harm. They wear amulets to protect them from this danger, and small babies are kept well away from public view so no one will see them and put the evil eye on them.

The other major group in northern Sudan is the Nubian tribes, who represent about 8 percent of the population of Sudan. They speak Nubian, an ancient language with its own alphabet and literature. Modern Nubians also speak Arabic.

The Fur

The majority population in the troubled Darfur region of Sudan are the Fur, a black African people. The name Darfur means "the land of the Fur." A smaller number of Fur also live on the Chad side of the border.

The Fur and a related group of African farmers called the Masalit are the main support for the SLA in its rebellion against the Sudanese government. They are also the main victims of the janjaweed and government troops in Darfur. Like the janjaweed, the Fur and the Masalit are Muslim, although their religious practices include many elements of animism, the ancient religion of their peoples. The Fur are also known to drink traditional African beer and eat pork, two practices that are strictly forbidden in Islam.

The Fur and the Masalit have their own languages, but many also speak Arabic when dealing with their Arabic neighbors and the central government in Khartoum. They live in settled villages where they grow millet, a kind of grain, chilies, potatoes, and sesame. They also grow cash crops—crops grown to sell or trade with others. Their cash crops include peanuts, onions, wheat, mangoes, and oranges. Among the Fur and Masalit, polygamy, or the custom of one man having more than one wife, is common. Polygamy is also a common practice among Muslims, whose men are often allowed to have up to four wives.

The Zabhawa are another African ethnic group who live in Chad and Darfur. The Zabhawa regularly make a twenty-seven-day trek across the Sahara to the Libyan border. There they sell their great herds of camels and trade for salt, a rare commodity in Sudan. The members of the Tallata Umboro tribe, in the southwest of Darfur, are unlike any of the neighboring tribes in their traditions and customs and are thought to have descended from the Fulani, a Muslim nomadic tribe from northern Nigeria.

The Nuba

The most populous of non-Arab groups in Sudan north of the Sudd is a dark-skinned group known as the Nuba. These people, whose interesting way of life and strikingly tall and dignified bearing have been the subject of many documentaries, are said

Displaced Sudanese women from the Fur tribe collect firewood as they make their way back to a temporary camp set up near Irly, in south Darfur in October 2004. The destroyed village of Irly can be seen in the background.

In Africa and parts of the Arab world today, slavery is not something in history books. It is alive and thriving. In Sudan, the Arab militias have been accused by both the United States and the UN of raiding black African villages to capture and sell slaves (*shown left*). Both the Nuba and the Dinka have fallen victim to slave raiders. According to *My True Story,* by Mende Nazer and Damien Lewis, a book published in 2004, the capturing of slaves was a part of the Arab war against the Nuba and Dinka. Nazer was a twelve-year-old girl in 1994 when the Arab militia raided her Nuba village. The raiders burned huts, slit throats, raped women, and kidnapped children. Boys captured in such raids, she writes, were often sold as cattle herders. The girls became domestic slaves.

The raiders took about thirty children, including Nazer, from her village. She ended up a slave in a house in Khartoum. She says she was made to live in a cramped shed in the yard. She ate only the family's leftovers and was constantly accused of being dirty and diseased. "Even the children were treating me like an animal," she writes. "Worse than an animal: Even dogs were patted and stroked."

Nazer managed to escape and tell her story, but she warns that slavery is still very much a problem in Sudan. "There is still slavery going on, right now, today," she writes. "I am an example and I am the living proof and it happened to me, personally. It happened to me in Sudan. . . . And I know there are lots of other people still enslaved in Sudan. I want people to realize this and that they need to do something to help stop it."

According to Anti-Slavery International, a private group, Sudan has "failed to take adequate steps to end raiding and slavery." The group claims that between five thousand and fourteen thousand people were captured and sold into slavery between 1983 and the present in the Sudan. The Sudan government has pledged to stop the slave trade, but both the United States and the UN continue to criticize Sudan for not doing enough.

From March 15 to April 5, 2006, a former Sudanese slave named Simon Deng led a walk from New York to Washington, D.C., to raise awareness of the continuing slavery in Sudan. Deng was joined on the walk by Manute Bol, the former basketball star who was born a Dinka in Sudan.

Nuba rattle-dancers with painted bodies entertained tourists in the past.

to be the descendants of people from the kingdom of Kush. Kush thrived along the Nile in Sudan more than three thousand years ago when Egypt to the north was ruled by pharaohs.

For thousands of years, the Nuba occupied much of the center of Sudan. When Arab tribes came to Sudan, however, they pushed the Nuba into the mountains, which are known today as the Nuba Mountains. For centuries after they adopted their mountain home, the fifty different tribes that make up the Nuba lived peacefully among themselves and with their

Arab neighbors. They kept cattle and terraced the mountainsides to grow grain, vegetables, and fruit.

Today, the Nuba are still mainly farmers, cultivating plots in the hills. Their main crops are beans, sesame, and sorghum, a kind of grain. Many Nuba practice an unconventional form of Islam that allows alcohol and pork, but many also practice Christianity and animism, even within the same family. The total number of Nuba is not known. In 1969 it was estimated at 1.5 million.

During the 1970s and 1980s, thousands of tourists came to the Nuba Mountains to see colorful Nuba tribal dances and wrestling. The government began a campaign to clothe the Nuba, since traditionally they wore little or no clothing. The government also tried to force them to follow traditional Islamic rules. After several years of such persecution, the Nuba declared their support for the SPLA. Since then, the government has reportedly given up its policy of "civilizing" the Nuba and has tried, instead, to wipe out their culture. Government troops have cut the Nuba region off from the rest of the world. They have killed the Nuba's animals and burned their crops. Whole tribes have been forced into camps where men and women are segregated, and there have been reports of government-allowed rape and genocide.

The Dinka

The Dinka, who number three million, are by far the largest ethnic group in Sudan and the largest group south of the Sudd. Although they speak one main language, they live in twenty or more tribal groups.

Most of the Dinka are cattle herders who move from place to place depending on the season. During south Sudan's rainy season, the Dinka live in villages of mud houses with grass roofs. During the dry season, all the village residents except for old people, ill people, and nursing mothers go with the cattle herd to camps. They do not return to the village until the next wet season, when the rain floods the riverside camps and turns the grasslands into swamps. The Dinka way of life revolves around their cattle. Cattle give them milk and butter. Dried cattle dung provides fuel to cook with and to heat their homes. They even use the ashes from cattle dung fires to decorate themselves and to make a paste for cleaning their teeth. They use cattle urine to wash with, dye their hair, and tan hides. The Dinka do not kill their animals for meat, but when one dies or is sacrificed, the Dinka then eat the animal's meat. They use its skin to make drums, belts, and ropes.

Social status in traditional Dinka society is determined by the number

FAST FACT

Slavery in Sudan has a long history. In ancient times, the Egyptians regularly enslaved prisoners captured in war during Egypt's many attempts to conquer the area. In 652, after the Arabs failed to capture Sudan, they signed a treaty with the Nubian kingdom of Makuria. Under the terms of the treaty, the Nubians agreed to supply 360 slaves each year to Egypt. In the following years, Sudan became perhaps the largest slave-trading center in Africa. Slaves brought from further south and west in the continent were sold at large markets in Khartoum to traders who resold them in Arabia and further north in the Middle East and Turkey. After the British conquered Sudan, they banned slavery, but their efforts to end the slave trade were only partially successful.

and strength of a person's cattle. A Dinka boy officially becomes a man when he is given his first ox and he takes a name determined by the appearance of the ox. The Dinka even make up songs about their cattle herds.

Many Dinka have converted to Christianity; many others, retaining the animist beliefs of their ancestors, believe that spirits inhabit the grasslands and also their cattle. The fiercely independent Dinka felt deeply insulted by the Sudan government's imposition of Sharia law in the south in 1983. They soon formed the backbone of the SPLA guerrilla army.

CHAPTER 3

Land of the River Kingdom

Sudan's history and culture are inseparable from the Nile River as it flows from the heart of Africa northward to its outlet in the Mediterranean Sea. Without the lifeblood of water from the river, life and civilization north of the huge southern swamp of the Sudd would hardly have developed.

There are two branches of the Nile: the White Nile, which begins in East Africa near the equator, and the Blue Nile, which begins in the highlands of Ethiopia. Lake Victoria, Africa's largest lake, is the source of the White Nile. Leaving Lake Victoria, the river is known as the Victoria Nile. The Victoria Nile flows into Lake Albert

An engraving published in John Speke's Journal of the Discovery of the Source of the Nile *in 1863 shows Ripon Falls in Uganda where the Nile flows out of Lake Victoria.*

Even though the Nile is the source of life and civilization for both Sudan and Egypt, it was not until the nineteenth century that the world learned the source of the great river itself. The Greeks and the Romans wanted to find the source of the Nile, but they were unable to penetrate the Sudd, the great swamp in southern Sudan.

In 1856, two Britons, John Hanning Speke (1827–1864) (*shown left*) and Sir Richard Francis Burton (1821–1890), undertook an expedition to East Africa to look for the river's source. They landed on the coast of Africa opposite the island of Zanzibar and discovered Lake Tanganyika. They were told of a larger lake further inland, but Burton, who was sick, could not make the trip. Speke went on alone and found the huge lake, which he named Victoria, after the queen of England.

Speke then returned to Britain and announced that Lake Victoria was the source of the Nile. Burton disagreed, arguing that the source was Lake Tanganyika. To settle the dispute, Speke, along with James Augustus Grant, went back to Africa. Grant and Speke traveled around the shore of Lake Victoria and found the Nile flowing out of it.

Burton, however, refused to accept Speke's evidence because he said that Speke had not followed the river flowing out of the lake far enough to verify that it was the beginning of the Nile. Burton and Speke were to publicly debate their arguments on September 16, 1864, but Speke died just one day before in a hunting accident. History, of course, has verified Speke's finding that the source of the Nile is, indeed, Lake Victoria.

and leaves as the Albert Nile. It then flows into Sudan, where it becomes known as the Bahr-al-Abyad, or White Nile, from the white clay suspended in its waters.

The Blue Nile (Bahr-al-Azraq) springs from Lake Tana in the Ethiopian hills. The Blue Nile then flows 850 miles (1,368 km) northwest to Khartoum, where it joins with the White Nile to form the great river simply known as the Nile. In ancient times, as today in Sudan, the Nile overflowed its banks once a year, depositing a rich layer of soil that made farming possible and provided a basis for early Egyptian and Sudanese civilizations.

Sudan today is a country with sharp ethnic and geographical divisions. Its history from earliest times reflects those divisions. From Khartoum north, civilization was closely linked to Egypt. This region, including the area between Khartoum and the Sudd, was called **Nubia** in ancient times. The region south of the Sudd has a recorded history of only a few hundred years.

The Kingdom of Kush

Excavations in northern Sudan show that humans built temporary settlements there along the Nile sixty thousand years ago. By 8000 B.C. a Stone Age people lived in fortified mud-brick villages on both sides of the river. They supplemented hunting in the grasslands and fishing in the Nile by gathering grains and herding cattle.

This civilization became known to the Egyptians as Kush. The first known Kush kingdom in Nubia was Karmah, which appeared around 2600 B.C. Karmah is named after the modern town of Karmah in Sudan where archaeologists uncovered the remains of a small ancient city. The city was built where Nile water could be easily channeled into low-lying farmland. The ruins of Karmah include a large cemetery, extensive fortifications, and two towers, probably used for grain storage and as watchtowers from

which the residents kept a lookout for the approach of enemies.

Karmah civilization was heavily influenced by the Old Kingdom of Egypt (2700–2180 B.C.), but it had its own identity and is generally considered the first recorded black African civilization. Most scholars think that the Kushites of Karmah were probably a mixture of black African and Egyptian races.

Trade with Ancient Egypt

Archaeologists have found much evidence of an active trade and cultural exchange between the land of Kush and Egypt. Caravans from Egypt carried grain to Kush and returned to the borders of Egypt laden with elephant ivory, incense, hides, and other goods from deep in the interior of Africa. The Egyptians particularly wanted the gold from the mines at Wawat, an area of Kush, and slaves, which apparently were plentiful further south in Africa. Slaves were needed as domestic servants and soldiers in the pharaoh's army. Traders could not send goods to Egypt by boat because of a series of **cataracts** in the Nile between Egypt and Kush. Once above the cataracts, however, the goods were loaded onto boats for shipment downstream to the great cities of Egypt.

For a while, the Egyptians were content only to trade with Kush. By

In this wall painting excavated from a site in northern Sudan, Kushites from the kingdom of Nubia are shown carrying gold, ivory, and animal skins to pay tribute to a high-ranking Egyptian official known as Rekhmire.

the time of the Middle Kingdom (2100–1720 B.C.) in Egypt, however, the Egyptians strengthened their military force in Kush. They constructed a series of forts along the Nile in southern Egypt and into Kush to guard the transport of gold from the Wawat gold mines.

About 1720 B.C. Asian invaders called Hyksos invaded Egypt and ended the Middle Kingdom. The Hyksos also cut all links with Kush and destroyed the forts along the Nile. Cut off from Egypt, the culture of Kush developed its own style of temples, pyramids, and cities. This culture was cen-

tered around the city of Karmah, on the right bank of the Nile. In 1630 B.C. the princes of Karmah were strong enough to invade Egypt itself and conquer some territory. The Karmah rulers were buried in large tombs, surrounded by hundreds of their court officials whose lives had been sacrificed to provide the kings with servants for the journey into the afterlife.

New Kingdom Invasion

After the Egyptians of the New Kingdom (1500–1100 B.C.) overthrew the Hyksos, they moved their armies into Kush and incorporated much of it into Egypt. Egyptian officials ensured the loyalty of local Kushite rulers by kidnapping the ruler's children to serve at the pharaoh's court. Kush became Egyptianized. Egyptian gods replaced Kushite gods. Temples were built in honor of the Egyptian god Amon. These temples remained the center of Kushite religion until the coming of Christianity in the sixth century A.D.

After Egypt's empire declined in the eleventh century B.C., Kush emerged as an independent power ruled from the city of Napata. About 750 B.C. Kashta, the king of Kush, conquered southern Egypt. His successor,

Painkhy, conquered all of Egypt and founded the twenty-fifth Egyptian dynasty. The Kushite dynasty lasted about one hundred years until the Assyrians conquered Egypt.

Rise of Meroe

In 590 B.C. an Egyptian army briefly conquered the Kushite capital of Napata. This forced the king and his court to move to the city of Meroe. For several centuries, the kingdom of Meroe developed independently of Egypt, which was ruled successively by the Persians, the Greeks, and finally the Romans.

An 1835 engraving shows the pyramids of Meroe, the fruits of hundreds of years of labor after the Kushites were exiled to Meroe in 590 B.C.

The rulers of Meroe followed the Egyptian tradition of building pyramids for their tombs. They dressed like the Egyptians, worshipped Egyptian gods, and built their houses and temples in the Egyptian style. They also built a well-managed irrigation system to channel the Nile's floodwaters. In the first century B.C. Meroe developed its own writing system using Egyptian script to express the Kush language. The ruins of Meroe today reveal a palace with baths and plumbing, factories, houses, and evidence of an iron-smelting works. It was a civilization based on farming the banks of the Nile, which were lined with farms and small towns. Small pyramid-shaped tombs held the bodies of kings and queens. A Lion Temple, still to be seen today, has exterior paintings showing the rulers of Meroe with the lion god.

In 23 B.C. a Roman army, intent on finding riches and other spoils of conquest, marched south and destroyed part of Meroe. The Roman commander, however, quickly abandoned the area because he thought it was too poor to bother conquering.

By the sixth century A.D. Meroe had disintegrated into three kingdoms: Nobatia, Muqurra, and Alwa. A Christian missionary sent by the Byzantine empress Theodora began preaching the Christian gospel in

> ## FAST FACT
> Theodora (500–548) was the wife of the Byzantine emperor Justinian I. The Byzantine Empire was a Greek-speaking Christian empire, the eastern half of the Roman Empire after 476 A.D. The Byzantines ruled Egypt as well as other parts of the eastern Mediterranean. Shortly before meeting Justinian, Theodora became a devout Christian. She sent missionaries to Sudan and other places to spread the gospel. Today, along with her husband, she is a saint in the Orthodox Church, commemorated on November 14.

Nobatia. Eventually the kings of the three Nubian kingdoms accepted Christianity as practiced by the Coptic Church of Egypt. The church sanctioned the kings' rule. In return the kings protected the interests of the church.

The Coming of Islam

The rapid spread of Islam began shortly after the death of the Prophet Muhammad in 632. Arab armies, inspired by the new religion, carried Islam north and east from Muhammad's homeland of Arabia. After conquering Egypt in 640 and what is now Libya, the Muslim armies entered Nubia in 642 and again in 652. They laid siege to the city of Dunqulah and destroyed its church. The Nubians fought fiercely, however, and forced the Arabs to withdraw.

The Christian kingdoms of Nubia were safe—for the moment. The Arabs abandoned their attempt to take Nubia by force, but Arab domination of Egypt isolated the Nubian church by cutting it off from other Christian countries around the Mediterranean. Islam made gradual, steady inroads into Nubia. Arab traders established markets in Nubian towns. Arab engineers operated Nubia's mines. Muslim pilgrims en route to the holy city of Mecca left from Red Sea ports in Nubia. In the ninth and tenth centuries, Arab Muslim tribes continued to migrate into the Nile Valley and mixed with the population. By the thirteenth century, Nubia was dominated by Arab culture and Islam. In 1276, the

FAST FACT

The Ottoman Empire, which ruled much of the Middle East, North Africa, and parts of Europe, lasted from 1299 to 1922. It was a Muslim empire run by the Ottoman Turks. At its height in the sixteenth and seventeenth centuries, the empire stretched from what is now Iraq to the borders of Austria in Europe, from Morocco in North Africa to the tip of the Arabian Peninsula. The ruler of the empire was the Turkish sultan, who presided in the Ottoman capital of Istanbul. After the 1600s, the empire slowly declined and lost territory. By the 1800s, although Egypt and Sudan were officially part of the empire, the Ottoman ruler of Egypt and Sudan acted independently.

Muslim rulers of Egypt ousted the last Nubian king and the region became subject to Egypt.

In the sixteenth and seventeenth centuries, many schools of Muslim learning were founded along the White Nile, and Sudan became known for its religious scholars. The region was also a center of Islamic mysticism. Mystics seek a direct emotional connection with God, often through meditation, singing, or sacred dancing.

Muhammad Ali Pasha

By the nineteenth century, Egypt had lost control of Sudan, which was now governed by an assortment of local chiefs and other rulers. In 1820, Muhammad Ali Pasha, the semi-independent ruler of Egypt under the Ottoman Empire, sent an army under his son Ismail to conquer the northern Sudan (as Nubia was now called) and bring it back under firm Egyptian rule. *Sudan* means "land of the blacks" in Arabic. Muhammad Ali, like the ancient pharaohs, was chiefly interested in the slaves and gold that Sudan could provide. Ismail easily defeated all opposition and soon Sudan came under Muhammad Ali's rule, with Khartoum as the province's capital.

The Egyptian ruler taxed the Sudanese heavily, and opposition to his government grew intense. The people rebelled in 1821, murdering Ismail along with his bodyguard. The rebellion, however, was quickly put down by fresh Ottoman troops. The next governor of Sudan appointed by Muhammad Ali Pasha reduced taxes and pardoned the rebels.

Slave Trading

In 1863, Ismail Pasha became the Ottoman ruler of Egypt. He wanted to conquer all of Sudan and extend his influence to the center of Africa. To do so, he needed a lot of money, which he borrowed from Great Britain and other European powers. Europe would give him the money, however, only if he worked to end the slave trade in Sudan. Slavery was thriving in Africa and in Muslim lands at the time. Sudan's Bahr-al-Ghazal region (now a state in the Republic of Sudan) was one of the world's major slave-trading centers. Long lines of slaves who had been captured by traders from all parts of Africa passed through the region. Most were destined for owners in northern Sudan, Egypt, and Arabia.

In 1869, Ismail Pasha asked Samuel White Baker, an Englishman, to lead an expedition up the White Nile to establish Egyptian authority in east Africa and to curb the power of the slave traders. Baker, a devout

Ismail Pasha, the ambitious leader of Egypt, was unable to keep Sudan under Egypt's influence, eventually abandoning his interest in the country in the mid-1880s.

Christian, accomplished both goals, but he alienated many interior tribes with his heavy-handed methods.

"Chinese" Gordon

In 1869, the Suez Canal opened, connecting the Mediterranean Sea with the Red Sea. For the British, the canal was a lifeline to Britain's colonies in Asia, particularly India. To defend it, the British sought to control Egyptian affairs even though Egypt was still officially ruled by the weakening

Ottoman Empire. The British exerted their influence on Ismail by controlling Egypt's finances.

In 1876, Ismail Pasha appointed a British general, Charles George Gordon, to be governor-general of the entire Sudan. Gordon was an English army officer who had won fame in China during the Taiping Rebellion (1851–1864). One of "Chinese" Gordon's first acts as governor-general was to put down a revolt in Darfur—by diplomacy. Some of the insurgents joined Gordon's forces and the rest fled south.

As head of the Sudan administration, Gordon worked to suppress the slave trade and improved the working of the government. Before his arrival, Sudan had a thriving trade in black African slaves run by Arab slave traders. Gordon, who was a devout Christian, was effective in limiting the slave trade, but he alienated many Sudanese who felt that he was launching a crusade against Islam.

The Mahdi

By 1880 Gordon, worn out by years of toil, resigned his position. In 1882, a serious rebellion broke out under a self-proclaimed Islamic messiah, or Mahdi, named Muhammad Ahmad. Muhammad Ahmad declared a **jihad** against the British and the Egyptians, who ruled Sudan. He convinced many

Muhammad Ahmad, also known as the Mahdi, is shown in this wood engraving from 1884. The Mahdi led a successful rebellion against Egyptian rule of Sudan in 1881, but the country would fall again, this time to British control, in 1899.

thousands of Muslims that he would drive out Christians and other infidels and establish a perfect Islamic society with the help of God. Ahmad's vast army of believers swept all opposition before it.

The British government sent Gordon back to Sudan to deal with the Mahdi. He arrived at Khartoum on February 18, 1884. He was warmly

The Mahdi

Muhammad Ahmad (1844–1885), later known as the Mahdi, was the son of a boatbuilder who claimed descent from the Prophet Muhammad. Muhammad Ahmad was reportedly deeply religious as a youth. In 1861 he approached Sheikh Muhammad ash Sharif, a well-known Sufi leader, to learn more about Sufism. Sufism is a **sect** of Islam that places great importance on a direct, emotional connection with God. In 1871, Muhammad Ahmad's family moved to Aba Island in western Sudan, where he built a mosque and started to teach the Koran. He became well known as a pious teacher who promoted the virtues of simplicity and prayer as laid down in the Koran. He taught that Muslims who deviated from the exact words of the Koran defied God.

In 1881, after a vision, Muhammad Ahmad declared himself Al Mahdi al Muntazar, "the expected one," the redeemer of Islam who would change the world into a perfect Muslim society. The idea of the Mahdi does not appear in the Koran, but has been widely believed for centuries among many Muslims. Due to his magnetic personality, commanding presence, and great **piety**, Muhammad Ahmad persuaded many Sudanese that he was the Mahdi. They believed he would end the corrupt Egyptian and Ottoman government of the Sudan. Even after his sudden death from typhus six months after conquering Sudan, his followers considered him the bringer of justice and equality under God.

received by many tribes in the area who did not like the Mahdi or his followers. His first act was to send British and Egyptian women and children, along with the sick and wounded, back to Egypt by boat. About twenty-five hundred people had been removed before the Mahdi's forces closed in on the Sudanese capital. By March 18, 1884, Khartoum was surrounded by the Mahdi's army and a siege had begun. Gordon, along with the British and Egyptian forces, refused to surrender.

The situation of General Gordon and his forces in Khartoum was widely reported in newspapers around the world, and the British public called for a rescue mission. It took many months, however, for the British to assemble troops and attempt to relieve the city. They finally arrived in Khartoum on January 28, 1885, to find that the town had fallen two days earlier. Gordon had been killed on the steps of the palace and beheaded.

The Mahdi was now in control of all of Sudan. For the first time in centuries,

An artist's interpretation of the Battle of Omdurman shows the highly trained British soldiers (in red uniforms) in combat with the less skilled fighting force of the Mahdiyah army.

Sudan was ruled by the Sudanese themselves. The Mahdiyah (Mahdist regime) imposed strict Sharia law on all Sudanese. The Mahdi ordered the burning of religious and legal books because he thought they emphasized African tribal law at the expense of Sharia law. He made people declare that he was the divinely appointed representative of the Prophet Muhammad. Then, only six months after uniting Sudan, the Mahdi died suddenly from **typhus**. His regime was carried on, however, by three successors that he had appointed.

Return of the British

In 1892, Great Britain turned its attention to Sudan once again. At that time, European powers were busy carving up Africa into colonies and "spheres of influence." The British, worried about French and Belgian interests in areas around Sudan, wanted to reassert British control. In 1892, Field Marshal Horatio Herbert Kitchener led the Anglo-Egyptian Nile Expeditionary Force of 25,800 men, mainly Egyptians, along with a number of river gunboats, into Sudan. The progress of the force was slow, but on September 2, 1898, Kitchener's force met the Mahdiyah army in the Battle of Omdurman. Although the battle opened with a charge by the Mahdiyah's fifty-two-thousand-man army, it was not a close contest. At the end of five hours, the Mahdiyah army had lost eleven thousand soldiers and Kitchener only forty, with four hundred wounded. The British and Egyptians regained control of Sudan.

Anglo-Egyptian Condominium

Having conquered Sudan, the British now had to rule it. The solution: joint rule by Egypt and Britain. The Anglo-Egyptian **condominium** over Sudan was declared in 1899. The governor-general of Sudan was appointed by the ruler of Egypt but only from candidates chosen by the British government. The Egyptian and British flags flew side by side in front of all government buildings. From the first, though, the British dominated the condominium.

The first joint-rule governor-general of Sudan was Kitchener himself. He was followed by Sir Reginald Wingate, who governed Sudan from 1899 to 1916. Wingate gained the support of the people because he trusted the Sudanese and appreciated their culture. Wingate and his successors expanded Sudan's transportation systems and promoted widespread education.

One major impact of British rule that still plagues Sudan today was the British policy of dividing rule between the Arab Sudanese in the north and the Christian and animist tribes of the south. The British felt that this division gave them better control over Sudan by pitting one group against the other.

In 1902, the British established Sudan's first modern, secular (not based on religion) school of higher education, Gordon Memorial College. The college concentrated on educating Sudanese in European values, such as secular democracy. It developed a core of educated people who felt that Sudan should be an independent nation. Political groups,

FAST FACT

A secular democracy is one founded on democratic principles not connected to any particular religion. One of the main elements in most secular democracies today is freedom of religion—the right of people to freely practice the religion of their choice. In the United States, freedom of religion is granted in the First Amendment to the U.S. Constitution. The First Amendment states, in part, "Congress shall make no law respecting an establishment of religion, or prohibiting the free exercise thereof."

at first mainly made up of graduates of Gordon Memorial College, began to demonstrate for an end to British and Egyptian rule. By 1943, one of these graduates, Ismail al-Azhari, and his followers established Sudan's first political party, the Ummah (Nation) Party. The Ummah Party quickly gained the support of Sayyid Abd al-Rahman al Mahdi, the son of the Mahdi. Al Mahdi had inherited the loyalty of thousands of Sudanese who had followed his father.

In the early 1950s, agitation for independence spread across the African continent. Colony after colony gained its freedom. On February 12, 1953, the Egyptian government signed an agreement with Britain granting self-government to Sudan. In 1953, Sudan elected its first parliament. Sudan became an independent republic on January 1, 1956.

CHAPTER 4

The Struggles of Independence

When Sudan achieved independence, the country's new democratic constitution and parliament became symbols of a newfound pride. Democracy had triumphed and the future was bright in the minds of the European-educated elite who had modeled the country after Great Britain.

The triumph was short-lived. Democratic ideals were held only by a small minority of highly educated Sudanese. It did not take long before Sudan's baby democracy came under attack. The new democracy soon suffered from a declining economy, widespread corruption, and ineffective government.

Military Coup

On the night of November 16–17, 1958, barely two years after independence, the commander in chief of the Sudanese army, General Ibrahim Abbud, took over Sudan's elected government by force. He dissolved all political parties, barred assemblies of

General Ibrahim Abbud was the military dictator of Sudan between 1958 and 1964, after which he became president.

people, and closed down Sudan's newspapers. General Abbud appointed a Supreme Council of the Armed Forces to run the country.

A 1997 photo shows soldiers from the SPLA cheering before going into battle against the Islamic-dominated government of Khartoum.

Abbud's rule was widely accepted by the Sudanese people, who wanted security and economic stability above all else. The economy improved almost immediately. On November 8, 1959, Abbud achieved another widely acclaimed triumph. He concluded an agreement with the Egyptian government under which the Egyptians gave up all claims on Sudanese territory. Although Egypt had agreed to Sudan's independence in 1956, the Egyptians had not given up hope of controlling the country.

The Abbud government, however, reinforced the political and religious divisions in Sudan. It gave all the important government positions to northern Sudanese Arabs. The army officers under Abbud also promoted the spread of Islam and the Arabic language to non-Arabs throughout the country. In the non-Muslim south, Abbud changed the required school curriculum, which was based on British principles and taught by Christian missionaries. The new curriculum was to teach Arabic and Islam.

The Struggles of Independence | **35**

Between 1962 and 1964, Abbud expelled all Christian missionaries from the south.

Southern Resistance

Ever since independence, there had been armed resistance in the south against the Arab-dominated government. In 1963, students and teachers in southern schools went on strike. They took part in antigovernment demonstrations that the government quickly put down, causing a number of students and teachers to flee to nearby countries.

Full-scale rebellion erupted in the south in September 1963. It was led by the Anya Nya, a rebel army that believed only violence would get the Abbud government to treat the south with respect. The response of the government was to try to crush the rebels with even stronger force. Rebellion and discontent spread, however, from south to north. In October, students at the University of Khartoum held an illegal meeting (mass meetings had been banned by the government) in order to condemn government actions in south Sudan. Violent student demonstrations followed, and the disorder spread among the northern Arabs. General Abbud was forced to resign. A temporary government was appointed to serve until elections could be held.

Gaafar al-Nimeiri

In 1965, Sudan made another attempt at democracy when it elected a new parliament. As before, however, the politicians could not agree on how to run an effective government. The fighting continued in the south, the economy got worse, and discontent grew again. In 1969, a group of military officers, this time led by Colonel Gaafar Muhammad al-Nimeiri, seized Sudan's government by force. Nimeiri established the Sudanese Socialist Union (SSU) as the country's only political party.

On February 27, 1972, in Addis Ababa, the capital of Ethiopia, the southern Sudanese rebels signed a historic peace agreement with Nimeiri's government. For the first time since independence, the guns were silent and peace came to the south. The south received the government's promise for a major voice in governing itself. It was to have a separate legislature and freedom to teach religions other than Islam.

In September 1983, however, Nimeiri, now worried about the growing power of a political movement in Sudan called the Muslim Brotherhood, changed his approach to the south. He appointed the head of the Muslim Brotherhood, Hasan al-Turabi, to be Sudan's attorney general. Al-Turabi immediately began to modify the nation's laws to bring them in accord with Sharia law. This meant that all citizens, regardless of their religious beliefs, were bound by the laws of Islam. The southerners, most of whom were Christians or animists, opposed this, and the civil war reignited with greater violence than before. The rebels were led this time by John Garang, a U.S. economics graduate, who formed the SPLA. The government quickly lost control of the south and Nimeiri declared a national state of emergency.

Nimeiri sought to crush the SPLA by overwhelming military force, but all the army succeeded in doing was destroying the south's food supply. In 1983 and 1984, this destruction, along with a drought, resulted in a widespread famine. Many thousands of people died before aid shipments from all over the world arrived in the region.

In April 1985, Nimeiri was overthrown by yet another general: his chief of staff, General Abd al-Rahman Siwar al-Dahab. This time the new military government allowed elections that, in 1986, made Sayyid Sadiq al-Mahdi, great-grandson of the Mahdi, the new leader of Sudan. Al-Mahdi, however, proved a less effective leader than his grandfather. During the next three years Sudan was again plagued by instability, economic problems, and a failure to reach a peace settlement with John Garang's SPLA.

Al-Bashir

In 1989 the Revolutionary Command Council for National Salvation (RCC), led by Lieutenant General Omar al-Bashir, seized power from al-Mahdi. Al-Bashir, who still controls Sudan today, declared another state of emergency. He suppressed all political opposition and stepped up the war in the south. In November 1995, al-Bashir's government ended humanitarian flights to the south in a failed attempt to put more pressure on the SPLA. The RCC disbanded in 1993, but not before Bashir was appointed president. He was elected to the presidency in 1996 and was elected again in 2000.

At a rally for Sudanese President Omar al-Bashir in Khartoum in January 2005, a female member of the National Congress Party shouts "Allah Akbar," which means "God is the greatest," in support of peace in Darfur.

The Struggles of Independence | **37**

CHAPTER 5

A Cloudy Future

Since independence, Sudan has been plagued with many problems: drought, starvation, civil war, a collapsed economy, and widely condemned civil rights abuses.

Despite these crises, Sudan's foreign minister, Lam Akol, is optimistic. Not only has the war ended in the south,

he says, but Akol hopes that peace in Darfur is not too far off. Since 2005, there have been peace talks in Nigeria between the Darfur rebel groups and the Sudanese government. The seventh round of those talks began in 2006, and Akol says that "the two sides are closer than ever" over many issues

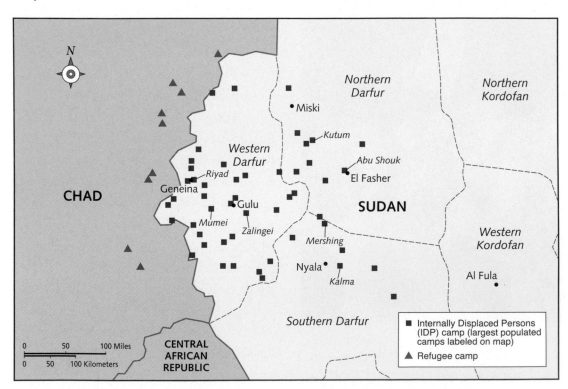

This map of the Darfur region of Sudan shows refugee camps where more than 1.8 million people who have been displaced from their homes are living.

on the negotiating table, including sharing power and the money from newly discovered oil fields in Darfur.

"Terrible Situation"

The actual situation in Darfur and eastern Chad, however, seemed to be getting worse, not better, by the end of March 2006. A poorly armed and undefended force of seven thousand peacekeepers from the African Union (AU) was increasingly unable to prevent the spread and intensification of the violence in Darfur. "You may have thought the terrible situation in Darfur couldn't get worse, but it has," said Peter Takirambuddle, of Human Rights

A Sudanese woman poses for a picture as she gets ready to leave a refugee camp in Northern Darfur in August 2004. Her possessions are loaded onto a donkey as she prepares to return home.

Watch, a group that monitors human rights around the world. "Sudan's policy of arming militias and letting them loose is spilling over the border, and civilians have no protection from their attacks, in Darfur or in Chad."

The Sudanese government was reportedly sending airplanes to bomb and kill civilians on the ground in Darfur and border regions of Chad. In 2005, the United Nations had declared Darfur a "no-fly" zone where such aircraft were banned. The International Rescue Committee estimated in March 2006 that five hundred people were dying each day in Darfur and eastern Chad.

Aid Crisis

The chaos of murder, rape, and cultural disintegration in Darfur is causing international aid organizations to scale back or leave the region. UN humanitarian aid chief Jan Egeland said that the fourteen thousand humanitarian workers in Darfur are now "hanging in by our fingernails." Egeland appealed for urgent international intervention before conditions worsen. "[The lives] of three million people are in the balance," he says.

Aid workers are unable to reach refugee camps and many fear for their lives. "There are attacks against humanitarian workers every week, again and again," said Egeland. "Our colleagues are being hijacked, harassed, and kidnapped. Our cars are being looted, and it's becoming routine. It's an outrage.... We're losing ground every day in the humanitarian operation which is a lifeline for more than 3 million people."

U.S. president George W. Bush called upon Sudan's government and the AU to agree to replace the AU force with a larger UN force of peacekeepers. Al-Bashir's government, however, angrily refused to even consider bringing in a UN force. Al-Bashir publicly warned that Darfur would be a "graveyard" for any UN force. Thousands of Sudanese supporters of the president took to the streets of Khartoum with signs reading "Death to invaders" and "Our country will be their graveyard."

Violence in Darfur will worsen and spread if UN peacekeepers replace the African Union force, said a senior Sudanese government official in March. "If the U.N. arrives, the troubles will spread in the region," Muhammad Elsamani, Sudan's minister of state for foreign affairs, told reporters. "Even if they send pure Muslim or Arab troops we will consider them invaders and will fight them."

Senator Clinton's Letter

In the United States, Senator Hillary Clinton (D-NY) wrote an open letter to President George W. Bush on March 16, 2006. She urged the president to step up U.S. pressure on the government of Sudan to stop the killing:

> Despite the work of the African Union, violence against civilians and aid workers in Darfur is increasing and spilling across the border into Chad.... The United States and the United Nations now possess extensive official accounts of the violence and, through a U.N. panel of experts and other sources, we also know who may be responsible. The Government of Sudan—reported by the U.S. State Department on March 8, 2006 to be responsible for the genocide in Darfur—continues to deny the existence of a crisis. It continues to threaten retaliation against an international intervention, and... continues to introduce additional military aircraft into Darfur.

FAST FACT

The African Union is an organization of all the African nations except Morocco. Its goal is to promote democracy, human rights, and development in Africa. It was established in 1963 as the Organization of African Unity (OAU) by thirty-seven independent African nations. The OAU mediated several border and internal disputes and was instrumental in bringing about majority rule and the end of apartheid in South Africa. The African Union replaced the OAU in 2002. The group now has greater power to promote African economic, social, and political integration.

Clinton went on to suggest a number of ways the United States could step up its efforts to prevent genocide in Darfur. These include appointing a special envoy, or official representative, to Sudan, to personally encourage peace talks; urging the UN to send a peacekeeping mission to Darfur; enforcing the UN ban on aircraft; and leading an international effort to punish those responsible for the widespread killing in Darfur. Senator Clinton's appeal was joined by a separate appeal from Nancy Pelosi (D-CA), the minority leader of the U.S. House of Representatives.

White House Concern

The Republican Bush administration does not often agree with Democrats like Senator Clinton and Representative Pelosi. On the urgency of the crisis in Darfur, however, both sides have reached some common ground. On February 16, 2006, Secretary of State Condoleezza Rice referred to the situation in Darfur as "genocide" and called for Sudan to accept UN peacekeepers. She said that the United States will consider creating a new post of special envoy to Sudan to accelerate an end to the continuing human tragedy there.

Deputy Secretary of State Robert B. Zoellick emphasized the administration's concern that urgent action is needed. "We don't have time to waste," he said. "There are heartbreaking conditions and they risk worsening. Millions of people are at risk here. We need to keep them at the forefront in our mind when we attend conferences. We need to provide security and food for these people.... Security is needed against rape and violence and against attacks from the janjaweed, rebels, and other groups."

Returning Refugees

Outside observers are also expressing concern over what has happened in south Sudan since the celebrations over the 2005 peace agreement. No

A Gambian soldier, a member of the AU peacekeeping force, stands at attention as Javier Solana (in white shirt), *the European Union security affairs chief, visits El-Fasher in western Sudan for talks with the AU's commanding officer about the security situation in Darfur in October 2005.*

new constitution giving more rights to the south has been written, and no action has been taken to begin to repair the war damage.

Millions of refugees from the long civil war in the south are expected to return to the area, with 500,000 expected in 2006 alone. According to international relief organizations, the refugees are returning to a devastated land that is unable to support a rapid increase in population. "The people of southern Sudan have not experienced significant improvement to their daily lives in the year since a peace deal ended Africa's longest-running civil war," said Jan Pronk, the chief UN envoy to the region. "For the people themselves in their daily lives, nothing has changed," he added, despite hundreds of millions of dollars in aid that has poured into the region.

Although Pronk told reporters that some "good steps" had been taken, he emphasized that there was still violence in the south, and that no discernible progress had been made in providing southerners access to basic needs, including education, health care, food, and clean water.

Rebecca Dale from the International Rescue Committee said that some refugees who had returned to their homes in south Sudan have since returned to the capital, Khartoum, because they found no way to support themselves. She said that 25 percent of the children in the south die before they reach the age of five, there are few schools, and there is only one doctor for every 100,000 people.

Malaria, an often fatal disease carried by mosquitoes, reportedly is a major problem in the south. And although there is peace, the violence has not stopped. According to the BBC, "thousands of armed men in militia bands still roam the countryside, preying on vulnerable travelers. There have been many accounts of rape and robbery."

Oil Discovery

Amid all the bad news coming out of Sudan, there is some good news: new oil fields have been discovered in Darfur and in the south. Sudan may have as much as 1 or 2 percent of the world's oil supply, enough to make it a rich nation in a world thirsty for oil.

Oil has already made a good friend for Sudan: China. China needs oil to keep its booming economy going, and the Asian nation now imports 7 percent of its oil from Sudan. China has also showered Sudan with $4 billion in direct investment over the past two years, with more to come. The Chinese are building oil pipelines and single-handedly rebuilding Khartoum.

Leaders in the south hope that Chinese money will also be used to rebuild the war-devastated southern area. The peace agreement in the south stipulates that the oil revenues should be shared equally between the south and the north. Negotiators at the Darfur peace talks in Nigeria were reportedly working on a similar distribution of oil revenues for Darfur.

Oil may also be the key to ending the centuries of warfare and destruction that have plagued Africa's largest nation. The fact that fighting in the south prevented Sudan from pumping more oil out of the region is widely credited with spurring the peace agreement there. Many experts think that oil could also bring peace to Darfur. Ken Bacon, president of Refugees International, told AlertNet, an Internet news agency, that oil could well end the fighting: "I hate to use this term, but oil should lubricate the peace talks."

On April 23, Osama bin Laden, leader of the terrorist organization al-Qaeda, undermined peace efforts and called upon Muslims to support the Sudanese government and to "prepare for a long war against [U.S. and European forces] in Sudan." On May 5, 2006, however, there seemed to be a breakthrough in peace talks for Darfur. On that date, the Sudanese government and the main leaders of the SLA signed an agreement to stop the fighting. The leaders of JEM and another rebel group, however, refused to sign the agreement and walked out of peace talks.

The people of Darfur still hope for peace.

When they flee the armed militias, Sudanese displaced people face terror, exhaustion, lack of food and water, and threats from disease. One highly contagious disease is caused by the bite of sand flies that live in the forests where refugees often hide for safety. In this photograph, a small boy sits beside his mother, who is receiving treatment for the desease at a clinic in southern Sudan.

Time Line

2600 B.C.	Karmah civilization arises in northern Sudan.
2100–1720 B.C.	Egypt's Middle Kingdom builds forts in Sudan and exploits gold mines there.
1500–1100 B.C.	Pharaohs of Egypt's New Kingdom conquer Sudan.
A.D. 500s	Sudan is divided into three kingdoms; Christianity is introduced.
632	The Prophet Muhammad dies.
640	Muslim Arab armies conquer Egypt.
652	Muslim army fails to conquer Sudan.
900s–1200s	Sudan becomes a Muslim country.
1276	Arab rulers of Egypt oust the last Nubian king and rule Sudan.
1820	Muhammad Ali Pasha sends his son to conquer Sudan.
1821	The Sudanese rebel against Egyptian rule.
1869	The Suez Canal opens.
1876	"Chinese" Gordon is appointed governor-general of Sudan.
1884	Khartoum is surrounded by the Mahdi's forces.
1885	A British-Egyptian force enters Khartoum to find Gordon dead.
1898	A British-Egyptian army under Field Marshal Kitchener defeats the Mahdiyah at the Battle of Omdurman.
1899	The British-Egyptian condominium is declared.
1956	Sudan becomes an independent nation.
1958	General Ibrahim Abbud seizes power.
1969	Gaafar al-Nimeiri seizes power.
1972	Nimeiri signs a peace agreement with southern rebels.
1983	Nimeiri breaks the peace agreement; civil war begins again.
1989	Omar al-Bashir seizes power.
2000	Al-Bashir is reelected president by 86.5 percent of the vote.
2003	Civil war begins in the Darfur region of Sudan.
2005	The Darfur war spreads to Chad.
2006	The U.S. State Department accuses Sudan of "genocide" in Darfur; April: Osama bin Laden calls on Islamists to fight UN peacekeepers in Sudan.

Glossary

animists people who believe that natural objects and animals possess spiritual power

British Broadcasting Company (BBC) the state sponsored media of the United Kingdom

cataracts sections of fast-flowing water filled with rocks, small islands, and shallow areas

civil war a war between two different groups of people who live in the same country

condominium joint rule over a territory

coup sudden action taken to achieve power

depopulated empty of people

dignitaries people of high rank or position

genocide the deliberate destruction of a whole race or ethnic group

guerrilla a soldier who does not fight in a regular army unit

infrastructure the roads, bridges, electric plants, and other things that allow a community to function

islamists Muslims who want a society based strictly on Islamic principles

janjaweed Arab militias fighting in Darfur

Justice and Equality Movement (JEM) a Darfur rebel group

jihad Muslim holy war

militias fighting groups that are not part of a regular army

missionaries people who travel to a foreign country to persuade others to convert to a particular religion

Muslims followers of Islam

mutiny a rebellion against an official authority

Nubia the former name of Sudan

piety devotions to one's religion

province a region governed as a political unit of a country, like a state

refugees people who flee to escape war or natural disaster, usually to a foreign contry. Because Sudanese are typically fleeing to camps inside their own country, their preferred description is Internally Displaced Persons, or IDPs.

savanna grasslands

sect a group of members of a religion who have separated from the usually larger, original group

sharia law based on the principles of Islam

Sudan Liberation Army (SLA) a rebel group in Darfur

Sudan People's Liberations Army (SPLA) a rebel group in the south

typhus a disease transmitted by fleas or lice

For More Information

Books

Bok, Francis. *Escape from Slavery*. St. Martin's Griffin, 2003.

Chapin-Pinotti, Elizabeth. *Phineas in Africa: The Sudan*. Oxford, UK: Trafford Publishing, 2005.

Diapiazza, Francesca. *Sudan in Pictures*. New York: Twenty-First Century Books, 2006.

Harmon, David. *Sudan: 1880 to the Present*. New York: Chelsea House, 2001.

Williams, Mary. *Brothers in Hope: The Story of the Lost Boys of Sudan*. New York: Lee and Low Books, 2005.

Web Sites

plasma.nationalgeographic.com/mapmachine/profiles/su.html
    Maps and information about Sudan from National Geographic

www.state.gov/r/pa/ei/bgn/5424.htm
    The most up-to-date information about Sudan from the U.S. Department of State Fact Book

www.sudani.com/dir/sudan-culture
    Information about Sudan's culture

www.sudan.net/society/recipe.html
    Menus and recipes from Sudan

Index

About the Author

Charles Piddock is a former editor in chief of Weekly Reader Corporation, publisher of sixteen classroom magazines for schools from pre-K through high school, including *Current Events, Current Science,* and *Teen Newsweek.* In his career with Weekly Reader, he has written and edited hundreds of articles for young people of all ages on world and national affairs, science, literature, and other topics. Before working at Weekly Reader, he worked in publishing in New York City and, before that, served as a Peace Corps volunteer in rural West Bengal, India.